12/03

## DATE DUE

6/02

| JUL 23 '02 | | | |
|---|---|---|---|
| OCT 14 '02 | | | |
| OCT 24 '02 | | | |
| NOV 08 02 | | | |
| DEC 14 '02 | | | |
| 2-14-03 | | | |
| | | | |
| | | | |
| | | | |
| | | | |
| | | | |
| | | | |
| | | | |
| | | | |
| | | | |
| | | | |
| GAYLORD | | | PRINTED IN U.S.A. |

*But if the archangel now, perilous, from behind the stars*

*took even one step down toward us: our own heart, beating*

*higher and higher, would beat us to death. Who are you?*

~*Rainer Maria Rilke,* Duino Elegies, 2

# for love of
# ANGELS

*Katrina Fried & Melanie Random*

A WELCOME BOOK

**Andrews McMeel
Publishing**

Kansas City

For information write:
Andrews McMeel Publishing
An Andrews McMeel Universal company
4520 Main Street
Kansas City, Missouri 64111

Note: Every effort has been made to locate the copyright owners of the
material used in this book. Please let us know if an error has been made, and
we will make any necessary corrections in subsequent printings.

Produced by Welcome Enterprises, Inc.
588 Broadway, Suite 303
New York, New York 10012

Library of Congress Card Catalog Number: 97-73528
ISBN: 0-8362-5078-8

Attention Schools and Businesses:
Andrews McMeel books are available at quantity discounts with bulk
purchase for educational, business, or sales promotional use.
For information, please write to: Special Sales Department,
Andrews McMeel Publishing, 4520 Main Street,
Kansas City, Missouri 64111.

Printed and bound in Singapore by Toppan Printing Co., Inc.
10 9 8 7 6 5 4 3 2 1

In memory of
Viveca Lindfors, Anna Ostblom,
David Viscott, and
Aimee Kendall Richardson.
Our angels.

# Table of Contents

## THE ANGELS

*They all have weary mouths,*
*bright souls without a seam.*
*And a yearning (as for sin)*
*often haunts their dream.*

*They wander, each and each alike,*
*in God's garden silently,*
*as many, many intervals*
*in his might and melody.*

*Only when they spread their wings*
*they waken a great wind through the land:*
*as though with his broad sculptor-hands*
*God was turning*
*the leaves of the dark book of the Beginning.*

~RAINER MARIA RILKE

# Introduction

What are angels? It is as timeless and unanswerable a question as pondering the origins of mankind. Depending on the experience of the believer, angels can be messengers, guardians, spiritual guides, or comfort givers. In the Bible they play a range of roles from lion tamer to recruiter. Their form, too, is as mysterious as their purpose. Modern angels take on as many shapes as there are people who believe in them. Sophy Burnham, author of *A Book of Angels,* describes an angel in the form of a Jamaican woman appearing to her at her mother's deathbed. In another angelic encounter a husband and

wife walking in the woods discover a cluster of beautiful winged women floating among the trees. An entire platoon of Allied World War I soldiers reported seeing angels wearing threads of gold with expanded wings that appeared as bright shiny clouds on the battlefield.

Angels in modern dress have crossed all the boundaries of religious preference, race, sex, and class. Angelic faith is no longer contingent upon a belief in God as it has been in the past, although the two often go hand in hand. This re-imagining of angels has ushered in a new fascination in our celestial friends and caused an epidemic of angel fever.

"ANGEL": FROM THE GREEK WORD "ANGELOS," A TRANSLATION OF THE HEBREW

For the first time since the twelfth and thirteenth centuries, angels have entered our collective spirituality. Angels are in our homes, hearts, and literature; they're on our airwaves, supermarket shelves, and television screens. From napkins to night-lights, there's an angel for everyone. *For Love of Angels* celebrates this loving fascination with our winged emissaries and explores this flourishing celestial world.

*Who has not found the Heaven -below -*

*Will fail of it above -*

*For Angels rent the House next to ours,*

*Wherever we remove -*

*—Emily Dickinson*

WE LOOK AT IT AND WE DO NOT SEE IT;

Its name is The Invisible.

WE LISTEN TO IT AND DO NOT HEAR IT;

Its name is The Inaudible.

WE TOUCH IT AND DO NOT FIND IT;

Its name is The Subtle.

~Lao-Tzu, Tao Te Ching, 14

The existence of angels is an essential element to the four monotheistic religions of the western world: Christianity, Islam, Judaism, and Zoroastrianism. The sacred texts belonging to these faiths teach their followers that angels are as real as the God they serve; to believe anything thing else would be a challenge to the word of God.

A faith in angels can also come from directly experiencing their presence. Angelic encounters have made believers out of even the most dedicated skeptics. Sophy Burnham, who wrote two books detailing dozens of real-life human encounters with angels, admits that the only way to believe truly is to experience angels for oneself: "... it seems perfectly correct to disbelieve in a Higher Power until you've got some proof ... We are given senses to receive our information with. We are given experiences of our own. With our own eyes we see, and with our skin we

ABOVE: *Detail from* Madonna di Foligno *by Raphael, 1512.*

feel. With our intelligence it is intended that we understand. But each person must puzzle it out for himself or herself."

However, a 1993 *Time* poll indicates that of the 69% of people who believe in angels, only 32% have actually felt an angelic presence. This suggests that despite Ms. Burnham's contention that seeing is believing, there are a growing number of people who believe in angels without ever having experienced one. This can be partly attributed to the introduction of New Age spirituality into our popular culture. New Age is not in itself a religion and does not require a belief in God. New Age angels are higher powers, who may or may not be linked to God, and whose sole purpose is to help and guide us through this life. In the New Age philosophy, one may adopt a belief in angels that is linked to a personal spirituality and sense of intuition rather than a religious belief or angelic encounter. This sentiment is reflected in the words of Swedish mystic Emanuel Swedenborg: "Do not believe me simply because I have seen Heaven and Hell, have discoursed with angels . . . Believe me because I tell you what your consciousness and intuitions will tell you if you listen closely to their voice."

The First Kiss *by William Adolphe Bouguereau, 1890.*

# The Nine Orders

In an attempt to understand the vast and rich world of angels, it helps to have a perspective on how they are organized and where they reside. The most common and accepted theory is that there are nine choirs or species of angels that encircle the throne of God. Originally conceived by the theologian Dionysius the Areopagite in the sixth century and later adapted by the Catholic theologian and philosopher Thomas Aquinas in the thirteenth century, the nine orders of angels are thought to bridge the gap between human beings and God. The first order is the closest to God, while the ninth order is the closest to man.

The closest to the throne of God are the Seraphim. These mighty beings are thought to be creatures of pure love and light. They show their endless devotion and love for God by perpetually chanting the song of creation, "Holy, holy, holy." Isaiah describes the Seraphim in the Old Testament as having "six wings: two covered the face, two covered the feet, and two were used for flying." The Seraphim tend to avoid human discord, visiting us instead in moments of quiet meditation or prayer. It is said that Lucifer descended from the order of the Seraphim.

The second of the nine orders, the Cherubim are the first angels named in the Bible as they are stationed by God at the gates of Eden to keep Adam and Eve from re-entering the Garden. It follows that the main role of the

*LEFT: Twentieth-century painter Marc Chagall portrays the prophet Isaiah encountering the Seraphim. The bright red and orange color represents the flames that are thought to engulf the angels of the first angelic order. OPPOSITE: This twelfth-century miniature shows the nine orders of angels surrounding the throne of God.*

Cherubim is as spiritual guardians. In ancient Assyria they were placed at the thresholds of tombs, temples, and palaces as protective spirits. The Cherubim are angels of knowledge and glory as well as guardians of the fixed stars. They are also the celestial record keepers and help carry out the will of God.

The Thrones are the third order of angels and are thought to be the ministering angels of justice. While the Seraphim and Cherubim exist in a purely immaterial spiritual realm, the Thrones are the first choir to border on the material world. They appear as the wheels covered with eyes that move the throne of God.

According to Dionysius, the Dominions, the fourth choir of angels, supervise the other angels and oversee the day-to-day happenings of the universe. They are also known to manifest the majesty of God. Legend has it that each nation has a guardian angel that is drawn from the choir of Dominions.

The Virtues rank fifth in the angelic hierarchy and are the angels of grace and valor. Their principle function is to perform miracles on Earth. They intervene and infuse courage and strength in humans during moments of great fear or difficulty. The

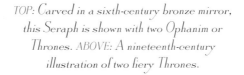

*TOP: Carved in a sixth-century bronze mirror, this Seraph is shown with two Ophanim or Thrones. ABOVE: A nineteenth-century illustration of two fiery Thrones.*

*Archangel Raphael descends to the earth.*

angels that accompany Christ to Heaven in the Ascension of Christ, for example, are regarded as Virtues.

The Powers, the sixth choir of angels, are said to be the first angels to be created by God. They police the Heavens in search of dark forces that might try to intrude upon the heavenly order. They are also believed to be the protectors of mankind against evil.

The seventh order of angels are the Principalities. They watch over the leaders of nations, inspiring them to make good decisions and share in the guardianship of those nations. In addition, they are protectors of religion and help to provide human beings with the strength to maintain their faith.

The Archangels are the eighth and one of the most well-known orders. Dionysius says that the Archangels are "the messengers bearing divine decrees." Depending on the source, this choir may consist of no fewer than four and no more than nine angels, although seven is the most commonly described. Of those seven, Michael, Gabriel, Raphael, and Uriel are generally agreed upon. The identities of the other three vary widely from source to source. Among their extensive duties each of the seven Archangels is assigned a day of the week over which to govern. The ruling Archangel of this order is traditionally identified as Raphael or Michael.

The Angels are the ninth order and the closest to human beings. They are essentially intermediaries between the heavenly realm and the earthly realm, between God and humans. It is from this group that the guardian angels emerged. They are certainly the most widely discussed and depicted order of angel and therefore the most well-known and recognized.

# Guardian Angels

The idea of guardian spirits dates back to early civilization and can be found in the belief systems of cultures around the world. The ancient Assyrians, Greeks, Japanese, Indians, and Egyptians are just a few examples of civilizations that had names for the individual spirits that watched over and guided every human being. The early Christian Romans even had different names for the spirits that guarded men (*genius*) and the spirits that guarded women (*juno*). The concept of guardian angels remained prevalent through the Middle Ages. The thirteenth-century religious thinker Thomas Aquinas strongly believed that each person had a guardian angel attending on him or her at all times. Judaism and Catholicism teach that each child born is assigned one or more guardian angels to protect and guide him or her through life's difficult moments.

Guardian angels have ascended to an even greater level of popularity in recent years. Countless books and artwork, even conferences and seminars, are being dedicated to proving their existence. But the real confirmation of the undeniable presence of guardian spirits can be found only by trusting the reliability of our own intuitions, our most spiritual instincts.

*LEFT: A detail from an ancient Greek vase (c. 500 B.C.) portraying a sphinx-like winged spirit offering counsel to a man.*
*RIGHT: A bronze Buddha statuette with two angels created during the fifth or sixth century in India.*

He will give his angels
charge of you,
To guard you in all
your ways.
On their hands they
will bear you up,
Lest you dash your foot
against a stone.

-Psalm 91:10-11

21

Oh sovereign angel,

Wide winged stranger

above a forgetful earth,

Care for me, care for me.

Keep me unaware of danger

And not regretful

And not forgetful of my innocent birth.

~Edna St. Vincent Millay

ften adapted by artists to reflect opinions of their time, angels have taken on many different shapes throughout the course of history. Contemporary angels differ greatly from their predecessors, and yet could not exist in modern form without a history from which to emerge. The beastlike Cherubim of ancient Assyria, for example, were replaced during the Renaissance with the prepubescent winged putti that came to be called Cherubs and have remained so popular and familiar through the modern era. What precipitated this change is difficult to pinpoint. One theory is that with the rise in popularity of angels during the Middle Ages, coupled with the artistic trends of that period, painters and sculptors began looking for more benign, cheerful, and less religious ways of depicting the angel. Young children and babies were more earthy and human than their cherubic ancestors, with the added virtuous qualities of total innocence and purity. That image of the chubby naked infant adorned with little white wings remains as popular today as it was in the seventeenth century.

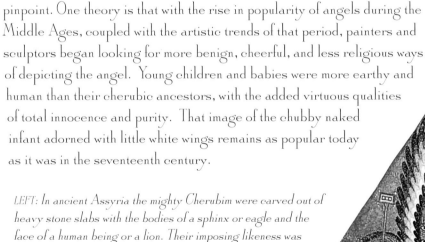

*LEFT: In ancient Assyria the mighty Cherubim were carved out of heavy stone slabs with the bodies of a sphinx or eagle and the face of a human being or a lion. Their imposing likeness was used to guard against evil at the entrances of palaces and tombs of important figures. RIGHT: By the thirteenth and fourteenth centuries, Cherubim had traded in their beastlike bodies in favor of a more birdlike frame with a human face and hands. Their change in appearance may be due in part to the writings of philosophical thinker Thomas Aquinas, who lived in the thirteenth century.*

ABOVE: By the fifteenth century, the Cherubim had completed their metamorphosis into the humanlike Cherub. Losing their fearsome qualities like multiple eyes and all but one pair of wings, Cherubs were given the likeness of sweet young boys.
RIGHT: The Cherubs' evolution would not be complete, however, until the liberal attitudes at the peak of the Renaissance allowed the little angels to be portrayed in the nude.

Though commonly thought of as an angel, specifically a Cherub, Cupid is actually the Roman god of love, often associated with the Greek god Eros. He is nearly always represented as a young, mischievous, winged boy carrying a bow and arrow.

Angels, in the early morning
May be seen the Dews among,
Stooping - plucking - smiling - flying -
Do the Buds to them belong?

Angels, when the sun is hottest
May be seen the sands among,
Stooping - plucking - sighing - flying -
Parched the flowers they bear along.

~ Emily Dickinson

# The Celestial Count

Depending on the source, the number of angels varies from 301,655,722 to more than 262,800,000,000,000 and every number in between. The former figure comes from the Kabbalists who made their computations in the fourteenth century. The latter finds its source in Islamic lore. According to the Talmud, every Jew is assigned eleven thousand guardian angels at birth. This figure doesn't even encompass the other eight angelic choirs. There is no official Christian position on the number of angels, although the Book of Hebrews in the New Testament describes them as "innumerable" and an old Christian children's poem specifies that each person has four angels assigned to him or her: "Four angels to my bed, four angels round my head. One to watch and one to pray, and two to bear my soul away." There are even differing opinions as to whether the number of angels is fixed or continues to grow with the human population. According to Church doctrine, angels are spiritual and therefore nonreproductive beings, but legend tells of angels that couple with humans, creating mutant offspring. Some New Age angelologists believe that additional angels come into being every day.

*It is said, and it is true, that just before we are born a cavern angel puts his finger to our lips and says, "Hush, don't tell what you know." This is why we are born with a cleft on our upper lips and remembering nothing of where we came from.*

~Roderick Macleish,
Prince Ombra

*OPPOSITE: Angels in the Saintly Throng of a Rose by Gustave Doré, 1860's.*

## The Fallen Angels

lthough there are a number of legends concerning the creation of Satan or the Devil, most agree that Satan was originally a highly ranked angel of God (chief of the Seraphim or Cherubim) who fell from His good grace to become the Prince of Darkness. The traditional story tells of the angel Satan challenging God's authority and omnipotence, resulting in his expulsion from Heaven. Another interesting account describes a group of angels known as the "Watchers," thought to be among the order of guardian angels, who were sent to Earth to aid in the creation of Eden and while there had sexual relations with the daughters of Adam. As punishment for this "sin of sins," God banished them from the heavenly kingdom to the fiery depths of Hell. Among these angels was Satanel who became the leader of Satanic forces.

*Satan has acquired a number of aliases throughout time.*
*The following is only a partial list:*
*Beelzebub, Azazel, Beliel, Duma,*
*Mastema, Gadreel, The Angel of*
*Rome, Asmodeus, Mephistopheles,*
*Lucifer, the Devil, the Beast, and*
*Iblis. In addition, he has been given*
*the more raunchy nicknames of Old*
*Horney, Black Bogey, Lusty Dick,*
*Old Nick, The Gentleman,*
*Monsignor, and Old Scratch.*

Black as the devil.
Hot as hell.
Pure as an angel.
Sweet as love.

~Charles Maurice de Talleyrand-Perigord's
recipe for coffee

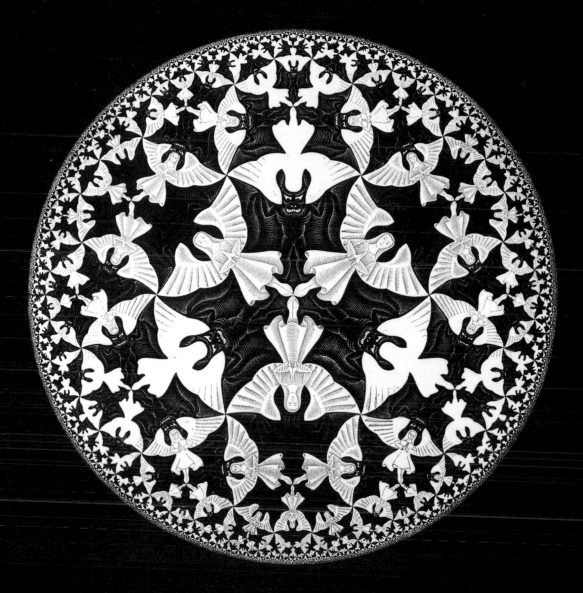

IF YOU'RE AFRAID OF DYING AND YOU'RE HOLDING ON, YOU'LL SEE DEVILS
TEARING YOUR LIFE APART. BUT IF YOU'VE MADE YOUR PEACE, THE DEVILS
ARE REALLY ANGELS FREEING YOU FROM THE EARTH.
—FROM THE FILM *JACOB'S LADDER*

THE DESIRE OF POWER IN EXCESS CAUSED THE ANGELS TO FALL;

he Seraphim mentioned in Isaiah 6:7 in the Old Testament are described as having six wings, yet Scripture does not support the notion that all angels have wings. In fact, rarely are they described with wings at all. So where did angels get their wings? Possibly the first depiction of a winged angel can be found among the artifacts of the ancient Sumerian city, Ur. However, it was not until the fifth century during the rule of Constantine, the first Christian emperor of Rome, that Christian angels began appearing with wings. In earlier Christian art, angels were depicted as young men with very human qualities. A mosaic in the Church of St. Prudencia in Rome may portray the first winged Christian angel. Of course angels were given the most beautiful set of wings possible, and artists modeled them after the wings of swans, geese, and eagles. Ever since then, wings have become the identifying attribute of an angel. It is generally believed that wings were added to signify the angel's ability to travel swiftly between Heaven and Earth. Their humanlike bodies represented their kinship to man, while their feathered wings suggested their celestial origin.

*ABOVE:* Saint Mary and the Choir of Angels, *from the Wilton Diptych, fourteenth century.*

ISLAMIC ANGEL JIBREEL IS DESCRIBED AS HAVING 140 PAIRS OF WINGS.

So many wings come here
dipping honey
and speak here
in your home O
God.

        *-Aztec poem*

Like living flame their faces seemed to
    glow.
Their wings were gold. And all
    their bodies shone
more dazzling white than any
    earthly show.

—Dante, The Paradiso,
Canto XXXI

The halo, the ring of light commonly depicted around the head of an angel, may have originated in the attempt of artists to represent the luminescent quality of the celestial beings. Halos came also to represent virtue and purity. They become a common angelic attribute in art after the fourth century.

# The Angelic Lifespan

The lifespan of an angel is a much debated subject. Both Jewish and Christian scholars generally agree that angels came into being during Creation, most likely on the first or second day. The early Catholic Church maintained that angels were immortal, and according to the Jewish text the Book of Enoch, angels are "not subject to death." However, the Talmud states that after their creation angels sing a hymn to God and then pass on at night only to be reborn the next morning.

The angels keep their ancient places—

Turn but a stone, and start a wing!

'Tis ye, 'tis your estranged faces,

That miss the many-splendoured thing.


— FRANCIS THOMPSON, "The Kingdom of God"

# Angelic Gender

While angels are almost always referred to in the Bible and other religious canons in the masculine, they have frequently been depicted in art as female. Those who claim to have met or seen an angel just as often describe the celestial being as female as they do male, depending upon the particular encounter. The most commonly held belief by theologians is that angels are neither male nor female; they are without gender. According to the Catholic Church, angels are "purely spiritual beings" who can take on any form they choose when appearing to humans. The Jewish text the Zohar reaffirms this notion by stating that angels "turn themselves into different shapes, being sometimes female and sometimes male."

*LEFT: The only archangel commonly portrayed as a woman is Gabriel. OPPOSITE, Two Angels, by Charles François Sellier, late nineteenth century. RIGHT: Archangel Michael, nearly always depicted as a male, is renowned for his prowess as a warrior and is often shown armed with a weapon.*

# MARY'S DREAM

winged women was saying
"full of grace" and like.
was light beyond sun and words
of a name and a blessing.
winged women to only i.
i joined them, whispering
yes.

—LUCILLE CLIFTON

# An Angel for Everything

Within the nine orders are hundreds of angels that govern and protect particular aspects of our universe and lives. Here is just a sampling of some of the angels that fill the heavenly choirs.

**GABRIEL**
In Jewish Kabbalah, it is not Gabriel but the Moon that is the angel of dreams.

**SAMANDIRIEL**
Samandiriel holds onto the prayers of those who ask his help until he perceives the time is right to act upon them.

| ANGEL OF: | | ANGEL OF: | |
|---|---|---|---|
| Air | *Chasan* | Life | *unnamed* |
| Anger | *Af* | Love | *Theliel* |
| Birds | *Arael* | Lust | *Priapus* |
| Chance | *Barakiel* | Memory | *Zadkiel* |
| Conception | *Laila* | Morals | *Mehabiah* |
| Dawn | *Lucifer* | Music | *Israfel* |
| Day | *Shamsiel* | Night | *Leliel* |
| Death | *Adriel* | Patience | *Achaiah* |
| Dreams | *Gabriel* | Peace | *Melchisedec* |
| Earthquakes | *Rashiel* | Plants | *Sachluph* |
| Embryo | *Sandalphon* | Poetry | *Uriel* |
| Fate | *Manu* | Pride | *Rahab* |
| Fear | *Yroul* | Prostitution | *Eisheth Zenunim* |
| Fertility | *Samandiriel* | Rain | *Matriel* |
| Food | *Manna* | Rivers | *Dara* |
| Forests | *Zulphas* | Silence | *Shateiel* |
| Free Will | *Tabris* | Sky | *Sahaqiel* |
| Future | *Teiaiel* | Snow | *Shalgiel* |
| Health | *Mumiah & Raphael* | Strength | *Zereul* |
| Hope | *Phanuel* | Thunder | *Ramiel* |
| Immortality | *Zethar* | Vegetables | *Sofiel* |
| Insomnia | *Michael* | Womb | *Armisael* |

**MELCHISEDE**
According to Jewish legend the angel of peace opposed the creation of Man and was burned by God punishment.

**ARMISAEL**
In pregnancy or may recite the fo lowing: "I conjur you, Armisael, angel who gover the womb, that you help this woman and the child in her bod

THE ANGEL ISRAFEL

In Heaven a spirit doth dwell
"Whose heart-strings are a lute";
None sing so wildly well
As the angel Israfel,
And the giddy stars (so legends tell)
Ceasing their hymns, attend the spell
Of his voice, all mute.

~Edgar Allan Poe, "Israfel"

EVERY VISIBLE THING IN THIS WORLD IS PUT IN THE CHARGE OF AN ANGEL.
ST. AUGUSTINE, *EIGHT QUESTIONS*

THE ANGEL OF LIFE

THE ANGEL OF DEATH

I looked over Jordan and what did I see?

Comin' for to carry me home

A band of angels, comin' after me,

Comin' for to carry me home.

——*"Swing Low, Sweet Chariot"*

*Swing Low Sweet Chariot by William H. Johnson, 1983.*

# Angels of the Zodiac

*The Zodiac sign of Virgo from* The Book of Hours, *fifteenth century.*

Just as there is an angel to govern every aspect of our universe, so too are there angels assigned to look over each sign of the zodiac. If the invocant knows the special rituals and incantations, angels of the zodiac, like all angels, can be called upon in ceremonial magic to perform different tasks. The chart on the opposite page shows each of the twelve astrological signs and the name of the corresponding angel.

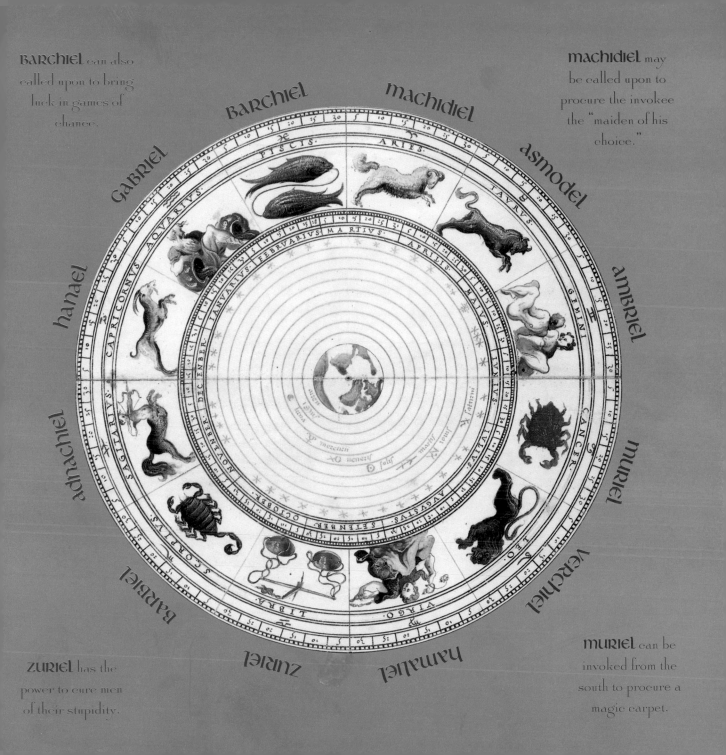

BARCHIEL can also called upon to bring luck in games of chance.

MACHIDIEL may be called upon to procure the invokee the "maiden of his choice."

MURIEL can be invoked from the south to procure a magic carpet.

ZURIEL has the power to cure men of their stupidity.

BARCHIEL

MACHIDIEL

GABRIEL

ASMODEL

HANAEL

AMBRIEL

ADNACHIEL

MURIEL

BARBIEL

VERCHIEL

ZURIEL

HAMALIEL

# Biblical Angels

ngels are referred to more than three hundred times in the Bible, although only three angels, Michael, Gabriel, and Raphael, are mentioned by name. Angels in the Bible perform a myriad of functions such as warrior, lion tamer, wrestler, recruiter, messenger, companion, advice-giver, and comforter.

Some of the most well-known and depicted biblical stories involving angels are:

ABOVE: *Annunciation to the shepherds from* Hours of the Virgin, *late fifteenth century. OPPOSITE:* Vision of Ezekiel, *by Raphael, 1518.*

- God's placement of the Cherubim at the gates of the Garden of Eden to guard against the return of the banished Adam and Eve (Genesis 3:24).
- The visit of the three angels to Abraham (Genesis 18:1).
- The angel interceding to stop Abraham from killing Isaac (Genesis 22:11).
- Jacob's dream of the angels on the ladder connecting Heaven and Earth (Genesis 28:10).
- Jacob wrestling with the angel (Genesis 32:22).
- Ezekiel's vision of God's earthly visit on the chariot made up of the fiery Seraphim, Cherubim, and Thrones (Ezekiel 1:4).
- The angel's protection of Daniel in the lion's den (Daniel 6:22).
- Satan's temptation of Jesus in the wilderness (Matthew 4:1).
- The angel advising Jesus in the wilderness (Matthew 4:11).
- Archangel Gabriel's visit to Mary announcing that she will give birth to the Son of God (Luke 1:26).
- The angel appearing to the shepherds (Luke 2:8).
- Michael's battle with Satan and Satan's expulsion from Heaven (Revelation 20:1).

DO NOT NEGLECT TO SHOW HOSPITALITY TO STRANGERS, FOR THEREBY SOME HAVE ENTERTAINED ANGELS UNAWARES.
—*Hebrews 13:2*

*Jacob left Beersheba and went toward Haran. He came to a certain place and stayed there for the night, because the sun had set. Taking one of the stones of the place, he put it under his head and lay down in that place. And he dreamed that there was a ladder set up on the earth, the top of it reaching to heaven; and the angels of God were ascending and descending on it.*

*—Genesis 28:10*

# Musical Angels

ngels are renowned for the sound of their ethereal voices singing in chorus praise for God. Not only blessed with vocal purity, angels are also accomplished musicians, masters of the flute, trumpet, and almost every string instrument. But angels are not only the makers of heavenly music, they are also the subject of many songs written and composed throughout history. Ever since words and music were joined together in song, angels and other heavenly dwellers have been a popular musical subject.

Angels we have heard on high,

Sweetly singing o'er the plains;

And the mountains in reply

Echoing their joyous strains.

–"Angels We Have Heard on High"

ANGEL'S TRUMPET:
*The common name for
Brugmansia, the beautiful
trumpet-shaped flower said to
resemble the horn that Archangel
Gabriel will blow on the Day
of Judgment. Angel's Trumpet
flowers from early summer
through the fall producing
fragrant blossoms. Don't let
its sweet smell fool you;
the buds are poisonous if eaten!*

Where the bright Seraphim in burning row
Their loud up-lifted angel-trumpets blow,
And the Cherubic host in thousand choirs
Touch their immortal harps of golden wires
With those just spirits that wear victorious palms,
Hymns devout and holy psalms
Singing everlastingly . . .

~John Milton, "At a Solemn Music"

THE FIRST DEPICTION OF

ANGELIC MUSICIANS IS IN

THE FRESCOES PAINTED BY

GIOTTO BI BONDONE

(CA. 1300) IN THE ARENA

CHAPEL, LOCATED IN

PADUA, ITALY.

# Modern Angels

In recent years angels have emerged from the spiritual shadows as highly regarded, eternally present, and unconditionally supportive higher beings. For the first time since the Middle Ages, when angels were thought to rule every planet, every shift in weather, every blade of grass, the celestial order has resumed its powerful presence in our popular culture. The seeds of this re-emergence of angels in contemporary society seem to lie in the fertile ground of New Age spirituality and modern evangelical Protestantism. The combined effect of the popularity of these two movements was an explosion of interest in angels at the beginning of this decade. But the angels of today are far more knowable and involved with the human predicament than their ancestors were. Indeed, the fiery, fear-inspiring Seraphim that occupy the order closest to the throne of God are virtually unknown to the average person. All that remains of the nine orders are the Angels and Archangels, the choirs closest to humans and farthest from God. In particular, contemporary society is primarily occupied with guardian angels. In fact, many modern angelologists believe that human beings can contact their personal guardian angels and even converse with them if they know how to summon their presence.

*Every man hath a good and a*

*bad angel attending on him in*

*particular, all his life long.*

~*Robert Burton,*
The Anatomy of Melancholy

# CONTACTING YOUR GUARDIAN ANGEL

There are different processes that one can use to summon the attention of angels.
The following is one meditative exercise used by the authors of *Ask Your Angels*:

1) Sit in your sacred space with your feet flat on the floor and your eyes closed.
Sense the presence of your angel drawing closer and closer to you.
Imagine that its wings are softly folded around you.

2) As you inhale and exhale slowly, feel or sense the presence of your angel reaching
out to you. Breathe in this closeness and let a question rise up within you.

3) Bring your attention to your heart. Place the question you want to ask in
your heart by visualizing the words written there.

4) When you feel the words in your heart, open your eyes and write the
question down in your notebook. Close your eyes again.

5) With the words of your question in your heart and in your mind, connect to your
deep desire to hear the voice of your angel. Listen in your heart and in your throat. Be
aware of any feelings that come up. Angels reach us through feelings, so that may be
the first form of contact. Allow the feelings and be open to the words that arise.

6) Write whatever you receive, which may be words, images, or feelings.

7) Remember to thank your angel for the message.

8) Read over what you have received.

The Meeting by K. Martin-Kuri, 1982.

*K. Martin-Kuri, an angelologist and artist, encounters angels in a unique way. In a deeply meditative state, Ms. Martin-Kuri experiences the presence of angels who direct her on what images and colors to paint on the canvas. Most of her paintings are commissioned and her clients can request either a "guardian angel" painting or a "life destiny" painting. In either case, Martin-Kuri communes with both her guardian angel and the other individual's guardian angel in order to create the painting.*

# Angelic Encounters

There are more reports of humans encountering angels today than ever before. There is even a bi-monthly magazine dedicated to reporting angel sightings. Most of these encounters occur in moments of great danger or meditation, although angels have been known to appear at the most unlikely moments as well. What is common to every experience is that angels always have a specific purpose when they contact us. Real life stories have been published in countless books and articles, particularly in recent years. The following encounter is just one example of these miraculous meetings:

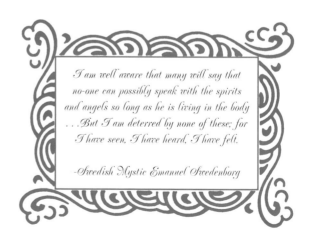

*I am well aware that many will say that no-one can possibly speak with the spirits and angels so long as he is living in the body ...But I am deterred by none of these; for I have seen, I have heard, I have felt.*

*-Swedish Mystic Emanuel Swedenborg*

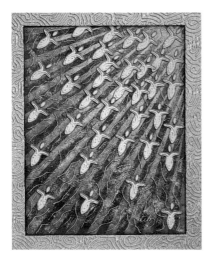

On New Year's Eve, 1986, a young man named Andy Lakey had a spiritual experience that irrevocably changed his life. On that evening, after excessively drinking and doing drugs, Andy stumbled home from a party and immediately got into the shower. He was overcome with numbness and a racing heart and thought that he was dying. He prayed to God that if He would let him live he would never do drugs again. As he began to lose consciousness, he saw swirling above him a bevy of angels and had the sensation that they were holding him in their arms. He woke up the following morning in a hospital bed, brought there by a concerned friend who had found him unconscious in the shower when he stopped by the previous night. Lakey accepted the overdose as a sign from his angels that it was time to quit drugs and alcohol and live a healthy life.

In December of 1989, three years after his near-death experience, he was visited again by three angels in his garage. At the time, Andy had just quit his job to become a painter. Inspired by his first encounter with angels, he felt a strong need to paint what he had seen and share with the world the love and power of angels. But he found himself frustrated and artistically blocked. That was when the angels appeared to him again. This time they instructed him to paint 2,000 paintings of angels by the year 2000. They promised to return when he finished the last painting on the final day of this millennium.

Andy began painting immediately and began receiving local attention for his original artwork. He soon added a three-dimensional element to his paintings so that they could be enjoyed by the visually impaired as well as the sighted. It was not long before his talent attracted interest from galleries and art dealers throughout the United States. He found his paintings being bought by important art collectors and even celebrities such as Peter Jennings and former president Jimmy Carter. Today, Andy Lakey has completed over 1,400 paintings, and is well on his way to reaching his goal of 2,000. The completion of his two thousandth painting will be celebrated in a special ceremony to take place in New York City on the evening of December 31st, 1999.

Black Elk Ascending with Spirits *by Standing Bull, 1930s*

I LOOKED UP AT THE CLOUDS, AND TWO  MEN
WERE COMING THERE, HEADFIRST LIKE ARROWS
SLANTING DOWN; AND AS THEY CAME, THEY
SANG A SACRED SONG AND THE THUNDER WAS
LIKE DRUMMING. I WILL SING IT FOR YOU. THE
SONG AND THE DRUMMING WERE LIKE THIS:
"BEHOLD A SACRED VOICE IS CALLING YOU;
ALL OVER THE SKY A SACRED VOICE IS CALLING."

—BLACK ELK SPEAKS

# Hollywood Angels

Hollywood has long been fascinated with the inhabitants of the heavens and their purpose and function on earth. Movie and television angels are almost always those of the guardian variety. In true Hollywood style, they are often depicted as handsome or debonair men, such as Cary Grant in the box office success *The Bishop's Wife* (1947) or Michael Landon in the hit TV series *Highway to Heaven* (1984-1988). However, the most famous Hollywood angel is far from dashing; Clarence, the aged, roly-poly, robe-wearing angel of the holiday classic *It's a Wonderful Life* (1946), has won the hearts of audiences around the world for over fifty years, despite his unglamorous appearance. A more recent film success about angels is the internationally acclaimed *Wings of Desire* (1988) by German director Wim Wenders. In this film two angels visit Berlin, observing mankind and reading their thoughts, until one of them falls in love with a human woman and leaves the angelic order. In 1996 alone, there were at least two major motion pictures released about angels, entitled *Michael* (starring John Travolta) and *The Preacher's Wife* (starring Whitney Houston and Denzel Washington), and one television series called *Touched by an Angel*. In a town like Hollywood, where stars fade more quickly than they rise, angels have exhibited what is known in show business as real staying power.

ABOVE: *John Travolta isn't your average archangel in* Michael. OPPOSITE: *In* It's a Wonderful Life, *Jimmy Stewart is sent his very own guardian angel named Clarence.*

"EVERY TIME A BELL RINGS, AN ANGEL GETS HIS WINGS."

—Clarence the Angel in *It's a Wonderful Life*    71

Angelic Spells & Recipes

## Angelic Spells to Win the Heart of a Loved One

Pour oil from a white lily  into a crystal goblet, recite the 137th Psalm over the cup, and conclude by pronouncing the name of the angel Anael, the planetary spirit of Venus, and the name of the person you love. Next write the name of the angel on a piece of cypress, which you will dip in oil, and tie the piece of cypress to your right arm. Then wait for a propitious moment to touch the right hand of the person with whom you are in love, and love will be awakened in his or her heart. The operation will be more powerful in effect if you perform it at dawn on the Friday following the new moon.

———

Place on the head of a girl's or woman's bed, as close as possible to the area where her head rests, a piece of virgin parchment on which you have written: "*Michael, Gabriel, and Raphael make* (the name of the person) *feel a love for me equal to my own.*" That person will not be able to sleep without first thinking of you, and very soon love will dawn in her heart.

—from *The History and Practice of Magic II*, by Paul Christian.

73

# Angel Hair Pasta with Tomato Basil Sauce

*3 tablespoons butter*
*1 tablespoon olive oil*
*1 small onion, chopped fine*
*2 cloves garlic, chopped fine*
*2 tablespoons red wine*
*1 lb fresh or canned tomatoes, peeled and chopped*
*salt and pepper*
*1 lb angel hair pasta*
*10-12 fresh basil leaves, chopped*
*grated Parmesan cheese*

Melt butter and oil in saucepan over medium heat. Add onion and garlic and sauté over low heat for 8-10 minutes. Add red wine and stir for 1 minute. Add tomatoes, salt, and pepper and simmer with the lid on for 15-20 minutes, stirring occasionally. In the meantime boil salted water for pasta. When water is boiling add pasta. Cook pasta for only a few minutes and drain. Add chopped basil to sauce and pour over pasta. Garnish with whole basil leaves and grated Parmesan cheese.

# ANGEL FOOD CAKE WITH VANILLA BUTTER CREAM FROSTING

## CAKE

11-12 egg whites
½ teaspoon salt
1¼ teaspoons cream of tartar
1 teaspoon almond extract
1 teaspoon vanilla extract
1½ cups sugar
1¼ cups cake flour

## FROSTING

8 o.z. confectioners' sugar
½ cup salted butter, softened
¼ cup milk
1 teaspoon vanilla extract

Preheat oven to 375° F. Combine egg whites, salt, and cream of tartar and beat until soft peaks form. Add almond and vanilla extracts, and slowly add sugar, continually beating until stiff peaks form. Sift the flour over the beaten whites and fold in bit by bit. Bake in an ungreased 10-inch tube pan for 30 minutes, or until a toothpick comes out clean. Prepare frosting by blending together the sugar, butter, milk, and vanilla extract in a large mixing bowl. When cake is completely cool, remove from pan and frost.

# The Angel Guide

The following is a select list of organizations, stores, publications, and on-line services dedicated to the topic of angels.

## Organizations

Angel Collectors Club of America
16342 W. 54th Street
Golden, CO 80403
*Sponsors conventions and newsletter*

HALOS
(810) 553-9111
*An organization devoted to
Helping Angel Lovers Own Stores*

Twenty Eight Angels
P.O. Box 116
Free Union, VA 22940
(800) 28ANGEL
*Provides information on angels;
has an angel hotline*

## Publications

Angel Times
4360 Chamblee-Dunwoody Rd.
Atlanta, GA 30341
(404) 986-9787
*Full color, bimonthly magazine
devoted to angels*

AngelWatch
P.O. Box 1397
Mountainside, NJ 07092
*Bimonthly newsletter, magazine,
and resource guide*

Angels On Earth
P.O. Box 1803
Vernon CT 06066-9874
*Bimonthly magazine that reports
real-life encounters with angels*

## Retail Stores

A Wing & a Prayer
2000 Riverchase Galleria
Birmingham, AL 35244
(205) 985-3569

Angel Presence
16783 Bernardo Center Dr., Ste. B
San Diego, CA 92128
(619) 674-4411

Angels for All Seasons
3100 S. Sheridan Blvd.
Denver, CO 80227
(800) 290-9941

Guardian Angel Shop
1018 Byron
Chicago, IL 60613
(312) 549-6804

Angel On My Shoulder
7011 W. Central, Ste. 132
Wichita, KS 67212
(316) 942-0088

Angelica
7 Central St.
Salem, MA 01970
(508) 745-9355

Angel Treasures
401 N. Main
Royal Oak, MI 78067
(810) 548-5799

Everything Angels
9 W. 31st Street
New York, NY 10001

Angels & Us
3257 SE Hawthorne Blvd.
Portland, OR 97214

Heavenly Treasures
5100 Beltline Rd. #248
Village on the Parkway
Dallas, TX 75240
(214) 980-2645

Guardian Angels
Box 391 Trolly Square
Salt Lake City, UT 84102

Unlimited Angels
1900 Esquire Road
Richmond, VA 23235
(804) 272-8893

CANADA
Angel Treasures
5905 Franklin Ave.
Niagara Falls, Ontario
(905) 374-6188

## *Mail Order Catalogs*

Angel Babies
25422 Trabuco Rd., Ste. 105-149
Lake Forest, CA 92630
(714) 855-4209

Angels Express
P.O. Box 8094
Gaithersburg, MD 20898
(301) 216-2638

## *The Internet*

Angels on the Net
www.magicnet.net/~netangel
*Angel information*

Ode to the Angels Marketing
E-Mail: angels@islandnet.com;
www.islandnet.com/~angels
*Angel products*

Sun Angels Innovations
www.sun-angel.com
*Angel products and services*

## *Angel Art*

Andy Lakey Art Studio
P.O. Box 696
Murrieta, CA 92564-0696
(909) 695-4130

K. Martin Kuri
Twenty Eight Angels
P.O. Box 116
Free Union, VA 22940
(800) 28ANGEL

# Literary and Art Credits

Pg. 1: Excerpt from *The Selected Poetry of Rainer Maria Rilke*, edited and translated by Stephen Mitchell. Copyright ©1982 by Stephen Mitchell. Reprinted by permission of Random House, Inc.

Pg. 2: *Angel*, Sir Edward Burne-Jones, Private Collection/Art Resource.

Pg. 6-7: Detail from *Venus at Her Toilet*, Louvre Museum, Paris/Art Resource.

Pg. 8: *Abraham Petitions the Three Angels*. Silvio Fiore/SuperStock.

Pg. 9: *The Angels*, Rainer Maria Rilke, from *Rilke: Selected Poems*, translated by C.F. MacIntyre, Copyright ©1940 C.F. MacIntyre. Reprinted by permission of the University of California Press.

Pg. 10: Detail from *The Virgin and Child*, Pietro Perugino, National Gallery, London/SuperStock.

Pg. 11: Detail from *Nativity*, Pietro Perugino, Galleria Nazionale dell'Umbri, Perugia, Italy/Art Resource.

Poem #1544 from *The Complete Poems of Emily Dickinson*, edit. Thomas H. Johnson. Copyright ©1929, 1935 by Martha Dickinson Bianchi, Copyright © renewed 1957, 1963 by Mary L. Hampson. Published by Little, Brown and Company in association with Harvard University Press.

Pg. 12: *The Pool of Bethesda* (detail). Joost Cornelisz Droochsloot, Christie's London/ SuperStock.

Pg. 13: *Madonna di Foligno*, Raphael, Vatican Museum, Vatican State/Art Resource.

Pg. 14: *The First Kiss*, William-Adolphe Bouguereau, Christie's, London/SuperStock.

Pg. 15: Ceiling Fresco, Andrea Mantegna, Palazzo Ducale, Mantua, Italy/Art Resource.

Pg. 16: Miniature of the nine orders of angels, from the Breviary of St. Hildegarde/Rheinisches Bildarchiv, Cologne.

Pg. 17: *The Prophet Isaiah*, Marc Chagall, ©ARS, NY Collection Chagall, St. Paul-de-Vence, France/Art Resource.

Pg. 19: Detail from *Madonna del Baldacchino*, Raphael, Galleria Palatina, Palazzo Pitti, Florence/Art Resource.

Pg. 20: Ancient Greek kylix, Museo Gregoriano Etrusco, Rome/Art Resource.

Buddha with two angels, National Museum, New Delhi/Art Resource.

Pg. 21: *Angels Hovering Above Jesus*, William Blake, Victoria & Albert Museum, London/Art Resource.

*Coat of Arms of the Silk Guild*, Luca Della Robbia, Orsanmichele, Florence/Art Resource.

Pg. 22-23: *The Birth of Venus*, Alexandre Cabanel, Musee d'Orsay, Paris/Art Resource.

Excerpt from "The apple-trees bud, Bud I do not" by Edna St. Vincent Millay. From *Collected Poems*, HarperCollins. Copyright ©1954, 1982 by Norma Millay Ellis. All rights reserved. Reprinted by permission of Elizabeth Barnett, literary executor.

Pg. 24: Cherubim statue, Louvre Museum, Paris/Art Resource.

Detail from *Celestial Hierarchy*, Duomo/Cefalu, Sicily/Art Resource.

Pg. 25: *Musical Angels*, detail from Pala dei Frari. S. Maria Gloriosa dei Frari, Venice /Art Resource.

Detail from *The Birth of Venus*, Alexandre Cabanel, Musee d'Orsay, Paris/Art Resource.

Detail from *The Abduction of Helen*, Guido Reni, Louvre Museum, Paris/Art Resource.

Pg. 26: "Angels, Angels, Angels." Andy Warhol, ©1997 Andy Warhol Foundation for the Visual Arts/ARS, New York.

Pg. 27: Poem #94 from *The Complete Poems of Emily Dickinson*, edit. Thomas H. Johnson. Copyright ©1929, 1935 by Martha Dickinson Bianchi, Copyright © renewed 1957, 1963 by Mary L. Hampson. Published by Little, Brown and Company in association with Harvard University Press.

Pg. 29: *The Saintly Throng in the Form of a Rose*, Gustav Doré, from Dante's *Paradise*/The Granger Collection, New York.

Pg. 30: *Satan In His Original Glory*, William Blake, Tate Gallery, London/Art Resource.

Pg. 31: *Circle Limit IV*, Cornelius Maurits Escher, Private Collection/Art Resource.

Pg. 32: *Fall of the Rebel Angels*, Limbourg Brothers, Musee Conde, Chatilly, France/Art Resource.

Pg. 33: *Hell*, Limbourg Brothers, Musee Conde, Chantilly, France/Art Resource.

Pg. 34: *Saint Mary and the Choir of Angels*, Flemish School, National Gallery, London/Art Resource.

Pg. 35: *Angel*, Abbott Henderson Thayer, National Museum of American Art, Washington D.C./Art Resource.

Pg. 36: *The Angel Standing in the Sun*, Joseph Mallord William Turner, Tate Gallery, London/Art Resource.

Pg. 38: Detail from *Madonna del Baldacchino*, Raphael, Galleria Palatina, Palazzo Pitti, Florence/Art Resource.

*Cupidon*, William-Adolphe Bouguereau, Roy Miles Gallery, London/Art Resource.

Pg. 39: *An Angel*, John Melhuish Strudwick, Roy Miles Gallery, London/Art Resource.

Detail from *Three Archangels with the Young Tobias*, Master of Pratovecchio, Gemaldegalerie, Berlin.

Pg. 41: *Heads of Angels*, Sir Joshua Reynolds, Tate Gallery, London/Art Resource.

Pg. 42: *Two Angels*, Charles Francois Sellier, Private Collection/Art Resource.

Pg. 43: Detail from *The Annunciation*, Pierre Auguste Pichon, Basilique Notre-Dame, Clery-Saint-Andre, France/Art Resource.

*Angel with a Sword*, Hans Memling, Wallace Collection, London/Art Resource.

Pg. 44: *Mary's Dream*, Copyright ©1980 by Lucille Clifton. First appeared in *two-headed woman*. Published by University of Massachusetts Press. Reprinted by permission of Curtis Brown, Ltd.

Pg. 45: Printed fabric, France circa. 1900, from the collections of Susan Meller, The Design Library, New York.

Pg. 47: *Angel Israfel*, Courtesy of the Arthur M. Sackler Gallery, Smithsonian Institution, Washington D.C.

Pg. 48: *The Angel of Life*, Giovanni Segantini, Galleria dell'Arte Moderna, Milan/Art Resource.

Pg. 49: *The Angel of Death*, Evelyn de Morgan, De Morgan Foundation, London/Art Resource.

Pg. 51: *Swing Low Sweet Chariot*, William H. Johnson, National Museum of American Art, Washington D.C./Art Resource.

Pg. 52: Virgo. Zodiac sign from the *Book of Hours*, The Pierpont Morgan Library, New York/Art Resource.

Pg. 53: Zodiac, with Atlantic Hemisphere at center, The Pierpont Morgan Library, New York/Art Resource.

Pg. 54: Annunciation to the Shepherds, from *Hours of the Virgin*, The Pierpont Morgan Library, New York/Art Resource.

Pg. 55: *Vision of Ezekiel*, Raphael, Galleria Palatina/Palazzo Pitti, Florence, Italy/Art Resource.

Pg. 56-57: *Jacob's Ladder*, Marc Chagall, Copyright ©ARS, New York Collection. St. Paul-de-Vence, France/Art Resource.

Pg. 58-59: *Angels Dancing Before the Sun*, Italian School, Musee Conde, Chantilly, France/Art Resource.

Pg. 60-61: *Angels With Musical Instruments*, Hans Memling, Museo Reale di Belle Arti, Antwerp/Art Resource.

Pg. 61: Detail from *The Last Judgment*, Giotto di Bondone, Arena Chapela, Cappela degli Scrovegni, Padua/ SuperStock.

Pg. 62-63: Blue tinted angel photograph, Alexandra Stonehill, Courtesy of Alexandra Stonehill.

Pg. 64: *L'Innocence*, William-Adolphe Bouguereau, Christie's, London/Art Resource.

Pg. 65: Excerpt from *Ask Your Angels*, written by Alma Daniel, Timothy Wyllie, and Andrew Ramer. Copyright ©1992 Alma Daniel, Timothy Wyllie, and Andrew Ramer. Reprinted by permission of Ballantine Books, a division of Random House, Inc.

Pg. 66: *The Meeting*, K. Martin Kuri. Courtesy of K. Martin Kuri.

Pg. 67: *Angel #1328*, Andy Lakey. Courtesy of Andy Lakey.

Pg. 68: *Black Elk Ascending with Spirits*, John G. Neihardt, Papers, Western Historical Manuscript Collection, Colombia.

Pg. 70: Film still from *Michael*. Photographer: Zade Rosenthal/New Line Cinema. Archive Photos/Fotos International.

Pg. 71: Film still from *It's A Wonderful Life*. RKO Radio Pictures Inc. Springer/Corbis-Bettman.

Pg. 72: *Christchild with Saint John and Two Angels*, Peter Paul Rubens, Kunsthistorisches Museum, Gemaeldegalerie, Vienna/Art Resource.

Pg. 73: Spells from *The History and Practice of Magic*, Paul Christian, ed. Ross Nichols. 2 Vols. New York. Citadel, ©1963.

Pg. 77: Putto with Violin. Baroque sculpture, Chiesa della Madonna, Novacella, Italy/Art Resource.

SPECIAL THANKS TO ...

Lena Tabori, Alice Wong,
Hiro Clark Wakabayashi,
Linda Sunshine, Natasha Fried,
and Matthew Webber.